A Tongue in the Mouth of the Dying

THE ANDRÉS MONTOYA POETRY PRIZE

2004, *Pity the Drowned Horses*, Sheryl Luna
Final Judge: Robert Vasquez

2006, *The Outer Bands*, Gabriel Gomez
Final Judge: Valerie Martínez

2008, *My Kill Adore Him*, Paul Martínez Pompa
Final Judge: Martín Espada

2010, *Tropicalia*, Emma Trelles
Final Judge: Silvia Curbelo

2012, *A Tongue in the Mouth of the Dying*, Laurie Ann Guerrero
Final Judge: Francisco X. Alarcón

The Andrés Montoya Poetry Prize, named after the late California native and author of the award-winning book, *The Iceworker Sings*, supports the publication of a first book by a Latino or Latina poet. Awarded every other year, the prize is administered by Letras Latinas—the literary program of the Institute for Latino Studies at the University of Notre Dame.

A TONGUE *in the* MOUTH *of the* DYING

LAURIE ANN GUERRERO

University of Notre Dame Press
Notre Dame, Indiana

Published by the University of Notre Dame Press
Notre Dame, Indiana 46556
undpress.nd.edu

Manufactured in the United States of America

Reprinted in 2013, 2014, 2015

Library of Congress Cataloging-in-Publication Data
Guerrero, Laurie Ann.
  [Poems. Selections]
  A tongue in the mouth of the dying / Laurie Ann Guerrero.
    pages cm. — (The Andrés Montoya poetry prize ; 2012)
  ISBN 978-0-268-01047-8 (pbk. : alk. paper)
  ISBN 0-268-01047-1 (pbk. : alk. paper)
  I. Title.
  PS3607.U463T66   2013
  811'.6—dc23
                        2012046210

∞ The paper in this book meets the guidelines for permanence and durability
of the Committee on Production Guidelines for Book Longevity of the
Council on Library Resources.

FOR DREW, VIC, & LIV, *always.*

CONTENTS

ACKNOWLEDGMENTS

Many thanks to the editors of the following publications in which versions of these poems have been published or are forthcoming:

Bellevue Literary Review: "Mr. G's Collection"

Huizache: "Pinedale, CA"

PALABRA: "My Mother Woke a Rooster" and "Ode to My Boots"

Anthology of Contemporary Tejana Writing: "The Alchemy of Mothering"

Acentos Review: "Preparing the Tongue," "Cocooning," and "My Mother Will Take a Lover"

San Antonio Express News: "On Blinding" and "Ode to El Cabrito"

Borderlands: Texas Poetry Review: "Put Attention"

Naugatuck River Review: "Wooden Box"

The Weight of Addition: An Anthology of Texas Poets (Mutabilis Press, 2007): "Las Lenguas"

Feminist Studies: "Babies under the House" and "Babies under the Skin"

Meridians: Feminism, Race, Transnationalism: "How I Put Myself through School"

Palo Alto Review: "Sundays after Breakfast: A Lesson in Cotton Picking"

Early versions of a few of the poems in this manuscript were also published in a chapbook, *Babies Under the Skin*, 2008 winner of the Panhandler Publishing Chapbook Award, selected by Naomi Shihab Nye.

8 ½" x 11" broadsides of "Preparing the Tongue," "Ode to El Cabrito," "Yellow Bird," "My Mother Woke a Rooster," "Sundays after Breakfast: A Lesson in Cotton Picking," and "Ode to My Boots" were created by printer Deborah Huacuja, each in a limited edition of fifteen. Original artwork by the author.

I am extremely grateful for the generosity and support of the Institute for Latino Studies/Letras Latinas at the University of Notre Dame, the Poetry Center at Smith College, my Canto-Mundo familia, and the elders at Alma de Mujer Center for Social Change.

Sincerest thanks to Francisco X. Alarcón, for your words, your fight, and your most gentle spirit. And to the man (and his family) for whom this prize is named, I give my heartfelt thanks: Andrés Montoya, whose commitment, whose passion, and whose tongue lives on in ours—whose name here, whose life here, gives me my name here, my life.

I would also like to thank Larissa Mercado-Lopez, PhD, for consulting my work for her dissertation, "I Feel a Revolution in My Womb: Mapping Cognitive and Somatic Transformation through Readings of Mestiza Maternal Facultad," along with Carmen Velasquez, Jane Velasquez, Atta Girl Productions, Lisa Cortéz Walden, Marco Cholo Quintet, Erik Bosse, Selena Sue Navarro, Monessa Esquivel, and Jesse Borrego for the adaptation of *A Tongue in the Mouth of the Dying* for a dramatic staged reading at Palo Alto College. Katherine Brown, thank you for your art and strength, and Deborah Huacuja for your generosity and belief.

Thank you, too, to Aracelis Girmay, Xelena Gonzalez, and Diana Marie Delgado, for the easing of my spirit, for your generous hearts, keen sight, and careful hands.

Unending thanks to the cultivators of my voice, my teachers and mentors: Annie Boutelle, Ellen Watson, Barbara Ras, Linda Harris, Irene Keller, Martín Espada (for the good fight), Ross Gay, Patrick Rosal, Joan Larkin, Ginetta Candelario, Michelle Joffroy, Jennifer Guglielmo, Sharon Seelig, Nikky Finney, Daisy Fried, Nancy Soporta Sternbach, Susan Van Dyne, Charlie Garcia, Mariana Órnelas, Rosie Castro, Alba De Leon, John Phillip Santos, Benjamin Alire Saenz, Naomi Shihab Nye, Norma E. Cantú, and Carmen Tafolla—thank you for helping me see who I am, what I can do.

Thank you also to Marta Lucia Vargas, Jonas Holdeman, David Crews, Roberto Carlos Garcia, Michelle Ovalle, Darla Himeles, Monica Hand, Yesenia Montilla, Kathy Engle, Elliott BatTzedeck, Lisa Wujnovich, Lynne McEniry, J. Michael Martinez, Leticia Hernandez, Luivette Resto, Millicent Borges Accardi, Carl Marcum, Juan Luis Guzman, Ire'ne Lara Silva, Sheryl Luna, Eduardo Corral, Francisco Aragón, Oscar Bermeo, Deborah Paredez, Carmen Gimenez-Smith, Celeste Guzman Mendoza—for being by my side when there is work to be done.

I am most humbled and grateful for my people, my village: Terri McBride, Anel Flores, Vincent Toro, Grisel Acosta, Celeste DeLuna, Amanda Baggett, Yolanda & David Rangel, Burt & Melissa Abrego, Carrie & Tony Blackburn, Sal & Maria Muñoz, Nanette Guadiano, Susan Q. Chavez; mis suegros, Gloria & David Garcés, Sr., Noel & Nina, and Marisa Reyes, la familia Garcés, la familia Navaira (Emilio IV & Diego for your spirit and commitment!), la familia Guerrero, la familia Cortéz; my Smithies & Northampton familia: Abe Louise Young, Antonia Bowman, Krystal Bosveld, Jeri Caska, Jen Barnard, Christina Eliopoulos, Jen Williams, Kimberley Rogers-Guimont, Jacqueline Guimont, Kendra Colburn, Jessica Quiroz, Kristen Norment,

Molly Fechter-Leggett, Megs Douglas, Frances Saunders, Judith Shumway, Mark Chappelle, Walt Colby, Gerardo Alicea, Jillian Flynn, and Erin Oliver (who knows my poems as well as I)—each of you have given me and/or my children your time, your space, your energy, your encouragement and support so that I could go to school, grow my children, grow myself, teach, write this book. My thanks are immeasurable.

Thank you, dad, for challenging me and for giving me your warrior spirit.

Thank you, mom, for teaching me what unconditional means.

War & peace incarnate, I love you both more than words could say.

To my grandparents, M. C. & Mary V. Cortéz, thank you for your history and for your love for each other.

For my beloved grandpa, Gumecindo M. Guerrero, who taught me how to tell a good story, raise tomatoes, walk tall, and for my brother, Gabriel A. Guerrero, my first and eternal protector—I am most grateful.

My love, David Garcés, thank you for giving me the support, the inspiration (x3), and the room to write. Every day you are a gift to me. And to my babies, Drew Garcés, Victoria Anne Garcés, & Olivia Jude Garcés, thank you for your unwavering love and patience.

I also wish to thank the late Adrienne Rich who, one afternoon in 2006 in Northampton, Massachusetts, after hours of talking about the battles one faces as a mother-writer, held my hands in hers and assured me of two things: 1) "you're a good mother," and 2) "you must never stop writing."

So very, very grateful.

INTRODUCTION TO THE POEMS

A Tongue in the Mouth of the Dying by Laurie Ann Guerrero is a stunning collection of moving poems. Here, poetry is both universal and very local; the personal turns collective in the mode of Tomás Rivera's Chicano classic . . . *Y no se lo tragó la tierra / And the Earth Did Not Swallow Him*. The authenticity and the plurality of the poetic voices strike the reader for their uncommon accomplished originality.

This is the poetry of both saints and sinners (and even murderers). The poet conjures up Pablo Neruda, Gloria Anzaldúa, Sylvia Plath, and is rooted in the best Latin American, Chicano/a, and contemporary American poetics, able to render an effective poetic version of Nepantla, the land where different traditions meet, according to Anzaldúa. These poems make the reader laugh, cry, cringe, lose one's breath, and almost one's mind, at times.

Tongue becomes the ever-present image. In the opening poem, "Preparing the Tongue," a cow's tongue is sliced in preparation for cooking, "I choke down / the stink of its heated moo, make carnage / of my own mouth, add garlic." The poet handles pen and butcher knife with the same great dexterity. Upon summoning up childhood memories, the poet pleads, "Open your jaws. / Let the eye of your tongue see . . . / how we licked fat black olives from tamales." Yes, here, poems become ultimately licking tongues.

A Tongue in the Mouth of the Dying is a collection of poems that will haunt readers and won't be easy to forget. I celebrate and praise the power of these poems that engage the great diversity of human reality with empathy, and do this, also with tremendous imagination. These poems restore my faith in the power of poetry.

—Francisco X. Alarcón,
Judge

To be a hero in undiscovered territories is to be obscure;

these territories and their songs are lit

only by the most anonymous blood and by flowers

whose name nobody knows.

—*Pablo Neruda*

PREPARING THE TONGUE

In my hands, it's cold and knowing as bone.
Shrouded in plastic, I unwind its gauze,
mummy-like, rub my wrist blue against the cactus
of its buds. Were it still cradled inside
the clammy cow mouth, I should want to enchant it:
let it taste the oil in my skin, lick
the lash of my eye. What I do instead
is lacerate the frozen muscle, tear
the brick-thick cud conductor in half to fit
a ceramic red pot. Its cry reaches me
from some heap of butchered heads as I hack
away like an axe murderer. I choke down
the stink of its heated moo, make carnage
of my own mouth, add garlic.

I.

ONE MAN'S NAME:
COLONIZATION OF THE POETIC

Bridges are thresholds to other realities, archetypal,
primal symbols of shifting consciousness. . . . [They] span
liminal spaces between worlds, spaces I call nepantla, a
Náhuatl word meaning tierra entre medio [land in between].
—Gloria Anzaldúa

i.

This is the womb   There are the men
From which my children came   Those white beards
This is the skin I use to feel. These feet   Wave like flags in the sky
                                                                        above us.

Walk the land. With these hands, I straighten
The spines of my children.
On this bridge

            they were given to live.

            There are the men who line up ships.

SUNDAYS AFTER BREAKFAST:
A LESSON IN SPEECH

There were no names for men like that—gringos
who stitched up their rules, their white garb, laced snug
the issues of the day: *Lord didn't make us to mix*

with them folk, they said. But God's got nothing
to do with black boys dumped still alive into a restless river.
God's got nothing to do with having to tell their mamas.

That bloody water ran through each dark vein across Texas,
fed the Gulf, all its brown-skinned people. This, grandpa could name:
los cuerpos—bodies swaying above the cotton like sheets on a line.

No importaba que no eras negro, pero que no eras gringo.
No, it didn't matter that you weren't black, grandpa says,
pushing himself from the table, but that you weren't white.

He lived his life this way: silent, like every man after him:
opening his mouth only to eat, holding his head above
the cotton, between white men and black boys.

BLUING THE LINENS

The white, which is the brightest of whites,
is one that has a slight blue hue.
—Mrs. Stewart's Bluing:
whitening since 1883

I read the book because it promised
to teach me. What I didn't know

was that whites don't start off white.
They're gray goods before the burning

bleach, before they bloom in red and turquoise—
embroidery on pillowcases, tea towels—

before grandma's napkins kiss your lips,
say *good morning.* Gray and yellowed,

a mass of brown, pure as dirt, in their cotton
bodies—a fibrous weave to swaddle

the butts of babies, soak up red wine,
wipe sweat between neck and nose,

the drip of infection. Nothing starts off white
as you know it. That kind of white takes bleaching

first, bluing ever after. White first.
Then blue. White, blue.

LAS LENGUAS

Once, a man told me
to hear the voice of God
one must first be able
to speak in tongues.

Years later, another man
told me speaking in tongues
was the kind of sin
you couldn't hide.

Who knows what the priest
told my mother when, with a quivering
chin, she pleaded, *Por favor, padre,*
necesito ir al baño, squeezing
her tiny, six-year-old thighs
together in the best English
she could muster.

SUMMER

In the birdhouse grandpa made for me when I was four,
life-sized, my name convex around the ovular door, I began.
A bird of squabble, my cawing unrecognizable

in a family of boars, I'd pick the burrs off the suffocating cactus
to decorate the red Velcro shoes my mother bought at Winn's,
queening my birdhouse where no one was ever allowed to enter.

Not even real birds. When my father hoisted my house
a good 3 or 4 feet up on rusted barrels made for gasoline,
I used my tricycle as a staircase—even decorated the handle

bars as if it were Christmastime with wilted morning glories and
yerba buena. I fell out once, nearly to my death,
trying to keep a runaway bull from noticing the blood

red of my shoes. I could not fly. It was in the dark gray summer,
when drops of rain began to fall, that I learned politics of men
and birds: we framed pictures of a black bull that played

in a pile of gravel that sat where my birdhouse used to.
I watched my house's red trim slant along the white plywood
walls smolder with the embers of a cleared brush in the early July

rain. How in the rain I loved it most. It was in the dark gray summer, when drops of rain began to fall, that I knew the human language: my body was not my own.

ONE MAN'S NAME:
COLONIZATION OF THE POETIC

ii.

The night we stood in a circle around you, a god,
poetry rising like fire to meet our mouths,
you asked about the babies I've birthed.
Wine-heavy, wise, gold-seeking
god, you redheaded Cortéz in a circle:
you ask about my babies, ask if they carry

one man's name.

The white hair on your chest fingers me closer,
your gold blood, gold chain, feathered serpent
in the skin of an old man: I waited for you: Wine-

heavy me, Malinchista.

A MEAL FOR THE TRIBE

Let me never go blind or get cut off
from the agony of learning.
—Sylvia Plath, Smith College, class of 1955

There is no eating without feeding, my mother

always said. The hunger is numbing.

I near enough to tease the tongue, sit at a table

with thin sheets of people and slip bursting,

purpled berries like rubies into a pouch on my lap:

crimson bombs in a seeping paper bag.

.

ONE MAN'S NAME:
COLONIZATION OF THE POETIC

iii.

Did you see me in San Antonio
at seventeen, my legs like the battle-worn door
of Mission San Jose: open: one baby St. Jude's,
one baby St. Andrew's, one baby fathered by the father
of St. Anne. Since my birth, they tell me
you are my father, your white mouth
teaching me how to speak: Cortéz.

Hail Mary.

       Blessed art thou amongst women.

YELLOW BIRD

for C. Hinojosa

She lowers her head: *Yo tocaba el acordeón.*
Quería cantar—quería ser estrella.
Instead she raised babies, a life
on her dark knees: La Virgen de Guadalupe,
San Martín de Porres, patron saint
of social injustice. Her pretty yellow wings,
all twisted and sore, she says all she wanted
was to play baseball like the boys,
spit truths like a cowboy, not pick cotton,
not master beady little French knots
for the wedding linens. We tell her to dance, sing
now with all her stomach, but she tidies
her feathers, hides her sharpened beak,
perches, like this, on a ring finger.

LITTLE MEXICAN POT

Filled to a sandpapery edge with bubbling love
potion: good beer, cilantro, fatty slab bacon,
sweet little beans spotted and brown as a newborn

goat. The stink of you can get a man going. Make him
weaken, wamble—meaty arms steady plateside
before he reaches for the first buttery bite.

Formed from the dry Mexican dirt, hand-painted
and hardened in fire, round sides, creased lip,
holes notched for fingers and dishrags.

A wide, red mouth that doesn't shut completely.

TURNIPS

We pulled them up—dug them out to let their white-purple skin see the sun. We dusted their tops and their bottoms like proud parents, our fingernails black with worm guts and hard gray dirt. One cool dusk, years ago, my brother and I planted them in one round row in the front yard where they could be seen. The small, smooth seeds were dark and jumpy in mama's hand like chocolate sprinkles on a cake. We giggled as we took two or three at a time and lulled them into the belly of their earth mommy. They grew quick. Overnight. I swear their limey-green arms welcomed us home from school the very next day. Then mama cut them, souped them. And we ate.

BABIES UNDER THE HOUSE

— — — — — — —

In Memoriam: Siblings,
Sariyah Garcia, fourteen months old
& Sebastian Lopez, four months old
San Antonio, Texas, March 2007

When you open your eyes again, Sariyah,
this'll just be one of those things—like rice and bean
                    tacos every night, having to go

          to the free clinic, buying gas with food stamps
          at Ben's Ice House at the corner of Pleasanton
          and Petaluma. But you know that, don't you—

know that your body will never grow completely?
When you open your eyes, your skin will be smooth
                    as the day you were born, not what it was

                    when they found you and the tiny thing
                    that was your brother. The dirt around you
                    will have licked away mother's milk

from your lips, absorbed the sour scent of mother's
breath on your neck. The iron-heavy taste of blood
          in your mouth, you won't even remember.

When you open your eyes again, Sariyah,
you will be the mother. Your tart Mexican heart
won't let you be anything else.

No need for grown-ups—Child Protective Services
who were too busy, the legislators who couldn't give
medication, education to this poor neighborhood,

this city, La Raza with no muscle, no voice. Hope
decomposing in a couple of plastic bags. But there are two
things you will have that your mother never did:

a whole Sariyah, a whole Sebastian.

ONE MAN'S NAME:
COLONIZATION OF THE POETIC

iv.

Let them rip the heart
from the fighting cock, stitch
their skins together tight to protect
the unexplored bridge.
Let them know the land, blood
that runs deep to its center.
Let them lead their brother.

Fight is the birthright of my daughters—two.

ONE MAN'S NAME:
COLONIZATION OF THE POETIC

v.

The night we stood in a circle
wine-heavy, you, our gold god,
fair-haired and bearded, you sacrificed
my children like the Aztecs

                              they are.

Line up the bearded men. Get in line.

ROOSTERS: HOMECOMING

for Yolanda Gonzalez Rangel

They're roosters! she corrects me. Chubby cocks hang above our heads from the ruffle of curtain in the room where her children eat. In her kitchen, next door to the house where I used to live, she laughs in two-step, pops a couple of XX con lima. *I've missed you, neighbor,* I say, peering through her window into the kitchen I used to cook in—next door—looking for the painting I left behind, the curtains I sewed, looking to see if I damaged the counters with an imprint of my ass, wondering if my DNA might show up if detectives ever needed samples: is my hair wound tightly in that carpet, skin flakes painted into that red door? Neighbor tells me the new woman next door has a baby that cries all night, and when the man struts home at 4 in the morning, he crows like a mad man. Our beer is ceremony. We talk about Maria: *Remember her? Her baby, Louis? Her husband? Did you know she was pregnant when he killed her? That he killed the boy first, in front of her?* Our children rush through the kitchen, paletas in hand, to the backyard with men who love us today. Passing the sal con limón, we pray for the woman next door, hoping blood is never shed in my old home like in Maria's two blocks down. Neighbor fluffs her curtains: *Come back,* she says. *Come back, and when you do, I'll bring you caldo the way I did when you were expecting la Chiquita, before you moved to the snow—where roosters are thin and don't know how to dance.*

ESPERANZA TELLS HER FRIENDS
THE STORY OF LA LLORONA

She killed her babies in the river over there by the Bill Miller barbecue place, you know, by the Holy Mother Church. She was friends with my grandma; they played bingo together, I think.

Oh, yeah, why did she kill 'em?

They were brats. And they probably never helped her clean house, and they were probably really whiney and always wanted candy in line at the H.E.B.

How'd she do it, Espi?

She drowned them one at a time, and herself, too, I think. That's probably why she cries. She probably didn't mean to kill herself, too.

That's not how the story goes.
My mom says it happened in Mexico,
not in San Antonio.

Shut up, Patty, what do you know?   Your mom's not even
Mexican like us. Anyway, I think she re'carnates herself. Or
maybe God doesn't want her in Heaven because she's crazy and
killed her own babies . . . but she keeps coming back.

Whatever, Espi.

Serious. She comes back in real life and keeps on killing her
babies. But, I don't think she cries anymore. She's so used to it
now. She's gone to Houston, to Hudson Oaks, to Plano, even
back to San Antonio, right here in the Southside.

You think you know everything—
tell us how come sometimes
she kills herself
and sometimes she don't?

I don't know. Maybe she cloned herself and now there're lots of
Lloronas. Maybe someone you know, Patty. Maybe your mother.

ODE TO EL CABRITO

More than sheep and cow
and butterfly, I love you.
No envy between us
like the rooster-footed.
In your belly, I live
like warm milk, goat-
thick and cloud heavy,
lick you from the inside
until the slaughter—when your mother
cries like my mother. When fire
sends its last breath to the stars,
I tear away your muscle, bubbling
fat, and warm tortillas over coal.
In the onion and cilantro,
you do not recoil like the burnt skin
of the pig, but spread yourself: sunbather.
The rest of you still on the spit,
gap-mouthed, your flesh-
less head tossed back:
you love being loved.
In the sweet meat of you—
little hooved, little horned—
I taste my own skin.

She was fat. Round as the moon,
just as gray. She didn't have time
for hiding, for safety, for hissing away
onlookers. Her legs jerked and out rolled
the little slick and wormy bundles. Two.
She circled them, inspected the mousy
ears, licked the furless pink skin.
They made no noise. Their tiny hearts rippled,
though softly. She ate one.
Then, she ate the other.

HOW I PUT MYSELF THROUGH SCHOOL

She has the refrigerator shelf labeled: *organic meats, caviar*
—the woman whose house I clean.

The wine rack, too, for the Chilean, Australian, French
chardonnays, sauvignons—so I'll know.

I sort her cupboards, her junk drawers: nail clippings, receipts,
catalogues, while her daughters, the underweight *darlings*,

stare as I reshelve their dolls and brand-new books. Stare
as their mother stares. Stare as I pour the ajo y cebolla

of my blood into a pot of rice that will end up in the trash
because of its spice. Stare as I shake the wrinkles out

of faded cotton panties and boxer shorts—the lingering heat
of the dryer taking me to a bedroom I never wanted to be in.

Sweat beading at the bridge of my nose, I accept the clothes
she collects in trash bags for my daughters, who are younger

but much bigger, knowing they will never fit, and wonder
how many times I'll have to slice the tongue out of my mouth,

chop my hands at the wrist, hear my babies ask,
Why do we take their used things, mama?

MORNING PRAISE OF NIGHTMARES, ONE

— — — — — — — —

No, it was not my daughter, the girl who swung,
noosed, from the rafters in my living room
above the scuffed wood floors. Blue-green armskin
swollen, wet, hung from the tunnels of her pink
tee. One rude, star-stamped Chuck still on,
the other flattened, down-faced, in the pooled liquid
of her body. There was no note, no mother
to claim the child, just poems branded onto her
rotting skin. No, my daughters were dancing,
living. And my mother, a frost of pink in her
skin, smiling, and younger than I am now,
pulled me, shaken, from the living room
to the grass, where she made it rain,
and told me to dance. And, I did.

MORNING PRAISE OF NIGHTMARES, TWO

When a steak knife fiddled against the sinew of my gut, I heard
the slow whine, felt each ridge, felt the simmering red erupt
like the juice of an overripe plum—the tickle of nectar running
down the body, still warm from the sun. And from the kitchen

to the street fair—as it often is in dreams—children laughing,
a clown, the color yellow, balloons melting against the burned
sugar of the skin. And guns—tiny, like from gumball machines—
in tiny hands. Bullets, red and green and gunmetal blue, piercing

the skin like botflies, their metal heads in deep until the offspring,
that winged blood, gently and timidly took flight. Then the peeling
of my skin: who was that crafter whose face I never saw?
That paper-maker, his teacup hands, his clothespin fingers

rinsing clean the lace of my forearms, the squared-off torso,
long sheet of leg, thick bit of finger and toe like strips of bacon,
strung up, decorating that red room like black and white photos
developing mountains or smiles or sex. I could taste my own blood,

though I couldn't lift my hands to finish the job—put myself
out of misery. I was but remains—a piled heap of slop
on the floor of a house I never shared a meal in. Even my eyelids
were gone and my spine exposed. I was an afterbirth without

the birthing, a too-early puppy whose whole pink body thumped
with each beat of his slow heart. This is my morning praise
of nightmares: *Open your eyes*, I hear three mouths whisper
against the flower of my skull, *mama, open your eyes.*

II.

SUNDAYS AFTER BREAKFAST:
A LESSON IN COTTON PICKING

— — — — — — —

South Texas, 1943

It was a kind
of dance: feet
shuffling in dust,

fluttering
hands like birds:
nest-building:

blood staining
brown birds red.
Cotton sacks, twelve

feet long,
dragging behind
like a tongue—

fat and slow
as sun.
I watch him:

slow weep
of his eye
remembering

the girl who'd name
and nurse
nine children.

He picks
my grandma
by the color

of her dress,
her eyes,
and because she's lucky,

not
by how much cotton
she can pick.

PUT ATTENTION

Put attention, grandma would say, as if attention
   were a packet of salt to be sprinkled, or a mound
     we could scoop out of a carton like ice cream.

Put attention, put attention. Put it where? In her hands?
   In the percolator? On top of the television set
     that seeps fat red lips and Mexican moustaches?

Next to the jade Buddha? Between La Virgen and Cousin
   Pablo's sixth-grade class photo—marshmallowy teeth
     jumping out of his mouth? We never corrected her.

Like the breast, Spanish lulled grandma's tongue, as we threw
   down shards of English, laughing, for her to leap in and around.
     Put attention, put attention. Put it where?

Shall I put attention in my glass and drink it soft like Montepulciano
   d'Abruzzo? Like Shiner Bock? Horchata? *Put attention.*
     Ponga atención, she tried to say in our language.

Put attention somewhere large. Back into her eyes.
   In the part of her brain that doesn't remember her own
     daughters, how to make rice, translate instructions.

ONE MAN'S NAME:
COLONIZATION OF THE POETIC

vi.

When you shove yourself into my throat,
the words I know become foreign, jagged.
A new race forms between the soft palate
and the base of my tongue. A pregnant mouth,
I carry you there, where words form:

I sew flags like babies.

BREASTS

It happens quickly.

Two pulpy, pink beads
swathed in skin soft as calf leather

rise, unfurling like a turquoise
spring. They are curious, pushy.

Not long before they take the reins,
manlike, no highway too bitter, no hand

too rough. Such resilient cups,
though raw against the scruff.

Most will tame

themselves, humble, swoop in a seasoned
bow, learn to fill up and empty out, calming

children, men. They'll wear, wilt—
sweet as burnt milk.

The tarnish can be rubbed away.
I leave mine. Evidence of easing

down the horse.

ODE TO MY BOOTS

Like San Antonio, bronze in the face, white
sky, timid green inlay of nopal, red flores.
I trace running stitch in swirl at the shaft,
finger the leathered sole. Like a shot of tequila,
you courage me up from the toes, delicate
grubs in tomato plants. You render me incognito
among men, ferocious among women who sit
cross-legged in their spiked disarmament.
With you, I navigate bridges; mi coyote on the border,
my twin lanterns. You wake in me the dormant cells,
the not-so-ancient history of Texas,
its women—slipping into something more:
vaquera, embroidered crown, umbilicus.
Both male and female—that knowing.

ODE TO A SKEIN
OF RED EMBROIDERY THREAD

Like the veined underleaf
of the New England maple,
but better. Slick, nuzzled
against your brothers, your sisters.
Brilliant head and feet curled
up like newborns, rosebuds
in anticipation. Revolution
in your six-stranded veins—
how I cherish you, envy you:
your potential, your ability
to become saint or star, bird or bear,
the name of a lover, mapped star
for the warrior, sprawling red palace
upon which the head can rest.

ONE MAN'S NAME:
COLONIZATION OF THE POETIC

vii.

My grandmother embroidered huipiles.
Named me the color of stone, lavender
in the sun. Wore a herd of elephants
on her middle finger, the baby always
almost dead. In white cotton thread on pink
cotton dress, she stitched swans to their heads,
made bloom red roses and white-flowered
Mala Mujer. She birthed nine children.
She sits now in a room where the faces are familiar
as snow and the hands that feed her are not her own.

She wears your name, a crown, Cortéz:
queen of a tongue no one understands.
What have you done?

WOODEN BOX

He demands this. Nothing
else. No mahogany slick,
or roses kissed by lilies. No
music or speech. Weeping,
limited. We are to file down
the aisle, nod head to his dead body,
return home to care for things
still living. We are not
to sob for the child
him, the bed- and alphabet-less
picker of cotton,
potatoes, tomatoes.
Follower of crops.
We are not to sob for the cactusman-
vaquero-lover him. Grandpa
who takes his milk from the moon,
who knows the time
for cookie,
the time for wine,
no.
When he is gone,
he will be gone.
*I can make the box
myself*, he says.
I can make it myself.

BLACK HAT

Gather your children. Make them presentable. Hide
your sin under new black hat. Come to my home.
Drink coffee. In my garden, rub mint

between your fingers, raise dirt to your nose—
let its purity make you feel pure.
Let your wife tell me to thank God

for what I have grown. Let her eye my children,
head tilted like a dying woman.
Sit inside. Let the crumbs of pan dulce

dot the faces of our children. Let them disappear
into a game for girls. Remove your hat;
tell me of your God, your new life.

When the ants come crawling out the top
of your head, let them rain down like tears.
Let the mass of little workers round your cheekbone,

explore the wound of your mouth.
Be a busy black mess. Let your red eyes be all I recognize.
Backed into a corner near a lamp, let the threads

of my voice tangle into a nest. Let the ants reach my legs
seeking the folds of my skin. When your tongue is ready,
say goodbye; let your wife and children grind ants

under their feet, smell the rot in your hair.
Scoop the ants back into the hat before you place it
on your head; let some trail you in my carpet like oil

or root themselves like seeds.
Say, *These are yours*, of the ants left behind.
Smear your wound on my cheek.

ONE MAN'S NAME:
COLONIZATION OF THE POETIC

viii.

Cortéz is my mother's name, too. Conquista,
the iron and arms she gave me to lock
myself up tight were stolen by the boy
who sells candy apples, bottled water
at the corner of Military & Flores.
He wears my armor under a new sun
                         and sweats in Náhuatl.

Grandma sees him in her dreams.

MR. G'S COLLECTION

In the CT scan, the tripas look like snakes
and one kidney dwarfs its once identical twin.

I see the lump, a wing bud, between his spine
and shoulder: *this is not the cancer*, says the doctor:

But tissue. A growth: Manteca: Fat.
Pregnant back full of children.

Collection of wounds, skinned over like a pie.
The many-cheated deaths: water for drowning,

horse hooves, guns, flipped up pick-ups,
booze to fill a young man's veins: flask. Cask.

All of it held up there: burden. World on his shoulder.
A monkey. Nest of wrongs, of worms. A blister.

Meatloaf. Coffee hardened to a brick.
Soap. Cake. A womb in which to grow

watermelon. A pot of beans. A dozen tamales.
He'll tell you it's a bag of money.

There, says the doctor, pointing
to what looks like the apple core we threw

off the jetties in the Corpus Christi Bay
when I was four, bobbing in grandpa's stomach

with each breath he takes: *there's the cancer*.

COCOONING

He's cocooning now, asked who would visit
as he chose a spot from which to hang
his wispy bed—from which to slip white silk
up from the creaking hinges of his field-worn feet.

His eyes rolled away like clams
into the ocean a good six years ago.
He works now, as always, with his hands.
This is the best way he knows.

In this state, the wrinkling faces of his children,
half a century old themselves & the white cotton sparks
atop the heads of his parents in the photo
near the front door, he sees only in memory.

Pregnant with himself, he crochets a mother sack,
adjusts his silks. His lean, east or west, according
to the sun. He pauses before enclosing the head,
his arms sleeved as a mad man, almost too heavy to raise.

He lifts his chin to smell the calling moon.
He takes blind metamorphosis
as he does his coffee: quietly
and in the dark hours.

BABIES UNDER THE SKIN

You come shy and unsure,
and we are strangers

but for the needing of each other.
I celebrate your births in water and wind.

Fish-mouths, rooting, even in death,
swallowing mouthfuls of air. Lipskin

papery, pink, wet, reaching to grasp
a nipple, a kiss. Your musty, meek fingers

reach for my hair—babies yearning
for mother muscle; my milk lets

at the thought of you. I stay living—
got to nourish the ones I can touch.

PINEDALE, CA

for my brother
in memory of Uncle Eddie

If you follow Aunt Eleanor to the back of the house,
you'll see the pomegranate bush we sucked from,
the olives puckering in five-gallon buckets. Open your jaws.
Let the eye of your tongue see what we have done here—
how we licked fat black olives from tamales, rolled them
up into the wide river of our mouths like cats licking
clean their babies. We can do this one summer,
with Uncle Candy and Uncle Eddie, and we can tell mama
the wine we drink from the jug in Aunt Esther's kitchen is juice,
and we can pick peaches and we can pick lemons and we can pick
fights with cousins we will never see again. And when they die
on the other side of the country, and we still have grandpa here,
we will pretend we're eleven and twelve,
sitting in the sun, singing rancheras
with old men who knew him before we did.

LIKE JESUS

for Q

We can bury the guns like gold,

under the grapevines—

in the earth, there are no fingers for triggers.

When the vines lay down their arms, bloom in grape

and tendril, and fruit hangs big as Texas like tongues

licking clean the air, we can gather revenge there—

pile it high, ready the stomp, make wine

and peace like Jesus.

WHEN I MADE EGGS THIS MORNING

for Jerry Rosalez

I broke them. Watched
them plop:
gooey discharge of egg
into a glass bowl.
Sprinkled them with salt
sucked from the sea,
pepper cracked with a twist—
tiny black skulls
flaked and dusted:
bonemeal. I beat them,
whipped them like a monster
until the line between yolk
and albumen was no longer
visible. I seared them
in a hot pan, toasted
the skins, served them
to my children. We ate.
I thought of you,
Roosterman:
the squawking birdmother
you shot by frying pan.

STONES

In Memoriam: Baby S
June 30, 2009–July 27, 2009
San Antonio, TX

I cocked my arm and threw it
flat—eye stone. Stone eye.
It never stopped, but sliced through,
cut crisp that edge of world veiled as sky—
a sheet, a cellophane drum, a skin,
ruptured. And there it was, my eye,
gritty and open

   and slowing now,
soft and rhythmic in its journey
like a ball about to stop but not
stopping. I could see the blinding white
where nothing exists: no up, no down
nor sound. No heat or water.
No growing. No human.
No law, no living. But a moon
melting, and a dog that barked
without voice standing on something
that cannot be named: a clear gel,
star effervescing. A cradle.
The piled bones of a fish,
and the piled bones of a baby.

And far off, away,
my stone eye rolled to a woman
hunched like an infected tree, her dead
head rocking in the bowl of her oaky arm.
In the flat palm of her hand, five
white stones: two of her own teeth
and three baby toe bones.

MY MOTHER WOKE A ROOSTER

She wasn't surprised that morning by the stove
when she cracked open a fresh brick of coffee
with hands feathered as the bed from which she rose.
She stood there. Upon her head, the morning sun
soothed her like guitars strumming—a halo: saint:
fit for lit candle on the mantle, the dressing table.

When she walked to the sink for water,
a bouquet of blue and black and rose
rose from the coccyx, up and over like a waterfall,
swiping the sugar and cream from the counter.
She was amazed by her wide presence in the tiny kitchen,
the incredible strength in her thighs, the ease of the strut.

In a pan hanging above the stove, she caught
the reflection of herself and swooped her rubbery
coxcomb back, letting it fall over her brow.
She pursed her red lips—her mouth just visible
deep inside a sharp beak.

She watched in wonder the staccatoed swivel
of her neck, rubbing what the night before
was the wrinkled throat of an old woman.
Her eyes now fitting on the face of a fighting cock.
Her red-tipped toes now claws and rough as a rope.

MY MOTHER ASKS TO BE CREMATED

No, she insists. After three funerals
with no body to view, no slack plastic
face to kiss one last time, no cold

gray hand in which to place a rosary
or belated letter of intent, she tells me
please and *don't forget*. She fears

her sisters will fight me. They will.
Some women have to see death this way—
the hard birth of death. Some

have to have the bloodless flesh
to grasp as they drop to their knees,
wailing. Some will use the death

the way they used the life. I say
give yourself to fire. I say let flames
take the soft bone. I say I promise.

MY MOTHER
WILL TAKE A LOVER

and devour him: hair, feet,
his toothy and crooked mouth.

By doing this,
she will devour herself.

Her hair will soften.
Her shoulders will thin.

When she tries to speak,
she will open her mouth

and the taste of him and her
together will be on her tongue

like a blanket of strawberries
long after summer has passed.

Though she will be invisible,
she will be content

to have tasted love like this.
Though he will be invisible,

he will have given
his life for her.

ANCIENT ALGEBRA

after Erin Margaret Oliver

I.

Danger − "brain" = me $\therefore$ ♀ + "brain" = dangerous

$\qquad x$ (bonemeal + modulation) = silence

x = {Fire, ♀}

If x = {Fire, ♀}, then $(x * \text{danger})^{\text{(DEGRADATION)}}$ = quest for "brain"

$\qquad$ Conquest + cotton + cactus − "brain" $\leq$ ♀

$\qquad$ God + milk + eyes − silence $\geq$ ♂

$\qquad\qquad$ {(Quest for brain)*(∞) = deprivation}

II.

♀ + ♂ = modification of the womb; bonemeal reconstituted

$\qquad$ ($\sqrt{}$ womb = ∞)

What you call my children $\neq$ what I call my children

$$\frac{\text{modulation (quest for brain + colonization of the poetic)}}{\text{my children}} = y$$

$\qquad y$ = revolution

revolution $\neq$ "education" + quest for equality

revolution + equality $\gg$ ("education")(∞)

$\qquad\qquad\qquad$ Solution = ∅

ONE MAN'S NAME:
COLONIZATION OF THE POETIC

ix.

Write the body well, I say.
Pink man, write well, write body.
Little pink man: write books,
write history, white history: Cortéz
and I have the same hands: grandmother.
Bodies ripped with babies and men: molcajete:
pounded, blood-red dust, pigment
for painting. Art. Framed in gold.

THE ALCHEMY OF MOTHERING

The pot boils gunmetal blue.
I hang my babies like shanks of meat,
smallest to largest. My butcher-

white apron smeared with child
mucus. A swab of sugar under the tongue
keeps their small bodies from coiling

like earthworms. The toes go first.
They do not cry. Metal permeates youth
quickly. They shine like chain mail.

They cool on the back porch, silvery
cherubs among roses and aloe.
It takes them months to learn

to move in their new bodies.
It takes all my life to see their faces
this way—my hands black and burned

through to the bone and scarred
by the imprint of eyes that are my eyes.
My science is the science of war.

EARLY WORDS FOR MY SON

You will probably make sense of it all some Wednesday
   afternoon as you sit with your wife and daughters,
      unbuckling leather footlockers, poems,

your mother's curvy schedule, knowing then
   why I never taught you anything but how to read
      and how to shade by crosshatching at the lip,

under the cheekbone, on the portraits
   you made of me. You will probably thank me,
      post-puberty, for never sitting down,

sparing you "the talk." You will learn the way I claimed to—
   some girl named Suzie who will also teach you to smoke.
      It took a long time before your father understood,

and who knows what the hell I'll tell your sisters.
   But you should know that when we were lonely,
      and you nine, wanting me to hold you,

I just couldn't do it with my arms. You were born male
   like I was born female, and all I've ever known
      is how to carry you in my teeth.

ON BLINDING

for Dave

When, finally, the shadows grow
like cactus, scraping the iris
grey as the sea, and I no longer see
the articulation of a bird's wing
or the curve of my own
magnificent knee, when finally
the nerve behind the bulbous
white, that tickle of brown, forgets
its job, loses its mind to time,
erupting hot and slow as magma,
know that I know the magic
of the blind: I have catalogued
your hands in my hands.

BIRTH DAY

for Aracelis Girmay & for Larissa Mercado-Lopez

> *I feel a revolution in my womb.*
> —*Cherrie Moraga*

Like the woman 59 years pregnant—
her child-tumor lost in the womb
and spread: all teeth and hair—
our mother-bodies protect themselves:
minerals and poems and love: stone.
Teeth do not unclench themselves
nor march back like soldiers into formation
of the mother's femur or spine.
The would-be toes in the womb scrape
muscle, stone up, calcify—what use is there
for a cactus & sun? A fig?
Wind to lift a dead bird's feathers?
Sometimes the birth day never arrives:
take a chisel—carve my face from my face.

One does not love a place the less for having suffered in it.

—*Jane Austen*

Opening epigraph from Pablo Neruda's *Confieso que he vivido: Memorias*.

"One Man's Name: Colonization of the Poetic": Epigraph from *This Bridge We Call Home*, ed. Gloria Anzaldúa and AnaLouise Keating.

"Bluing the Linens": Claims for Mrs. Stewart's Bluing taken from product website and label.

"Meal for the Tribe": Epigraph from *The Unabridged Journals of Sylvia Plath*.

"Babies under the House": The decomposing bodies of babies, Sariyah Garcia and her brother Sebastian Lopez, were found under their Southside San Antonio home in March 2007. Their nineteen-year-old mother, Valerie Lopez, was convicted of their murder and sentenced to life in prison.

"Roosters": In memory of Maria Moreno, her son Louis, and unborn child murdered in their home by Roland Moreno, husband/father, in a double murder-suicide—September 2003, Southside, San Antonio.

"Stones": In memory of three-week-old Scott Wesley Buchholz-Sanchez, brutally murdered and cannibalized by his mother, July 27, 2009, San Antonio. His mother, Otty Sanchez, was found not guilty by reason of insanity.

"Birth Day": Epigraph from Cherrie Moraga's *Waiting in the Wings*. The statement "Wind to lift a dead bird's feathers" is adapted from Aracelis Girmay's "I am Not Ready to Die Yet" from *Kingdom Animalia*.

End quotation from Jane Austen's *Persuasion*.

Photo credit: Drew Garces

LAURIE ANN GUERRERO is the author of *Babies under the Skin*,
which won the 2008 Panhandler Publishing Chapbook Award.
Her poetry and criticism have appeared in a number of journals.
She teaches for the M.F.A. Program at the University of Texas
at El Paso, University of the Incarnate Word, and Palo Alto College
in San Antonio, Texas.